LADY GAGA

A Little Golden Book® Biography

By Michael Joosten
Illustrated by Laura Catrinella

🌷 A GOLDEN BOOK • NEW YORK

Text copyright © 2024 by Michael Joosten
Cover art and interior illustrations copyright © 2024 by Laura Catrinella
All rights reserved. Published in the United States by Golden Books, an imprint of
Random House Children's Books, a division of Penguin Random House LLC, 1745 Broadway,
New York, NY 10019. Golden Books, A Golden Book, A Little Golden Book, the G colophon,
and the distinctive gold spine are registered trademarks of Penguin Random House LLC.
rhcbooks.com
Educators and librarians, for a variety of teaching tools, visit us at RHTeachersLibrarians.com
Library of Congress Control Number: 2023930098
ISBN 978-0-593-64732-5 (trade) — ISBN 978-0-593-64733-2 (ebook)
Printed in the United States of America
10 9 8 7 6 5 4 3 2 1

Stefani Joanne Angelina Germanotta, who one day would be known as Lady Gaga, was born on March 28, 1986, in New York City. The Big Apple has always been full of interesting and creative people—and Stefani grew up right in the middle of all that energy and excitement.

While she was learning to walk, Stefani's parents noticed that when she pulled herself up by the leg of the piano, her tiny hands would land on the keys. She would stand there and tap them over and over, listening to the sounds each one made.

Soon enough, her mother discovered that Stefani could hear a song, then play some of its notes on the piano. She realized her daughter had a very special connection to music, so when Stefani turned four years old, she started taking piano lessons.

Before long, Stefani wrote a song of her very own! It was called "Dollar Bills" and was inspired by one of her parents' favorite rock bands, Pink Floyd.

Stefani loved all the classical piano music she was playing, but when she was thirteen, her father asked her to learn a rock song by Bruce Springsteen. If she did, he would replace their small piano with a big one called a baby grand.

The song was "Thunder Road," and Stefani worked hard to learn it. When she finally played it for him, her dad was very proud. He kept his promise and bought the new piano.

Because Stefani listened to different music and wore different clothes, her classmates would sometimes make fun of her and say hurtful things. Being treated unkindly made Stefani not want to go to school.

But no matter how sad she felt, she still loved to be creative. Stefani was determined to keep practicing music, writing songs, and following her dreams.

As Stefani got older, she began performing in talent shows called open mic nights across New York City. She was still too young to be in some of the clubs where the shows were. So Stefani's mother would go along to make sure her daughter got a chance to perform.

At first, Stefani was nervous to play in front of crowds. But each time she got on a stage, her confidence grew stronger and stronger.

When she turned seventeen, Stefani was accepted into New York University's famous Tisch School of the Arts. But learning about the music other people created wasn't what she wanted to do. She wanted to make her own music.

Inspired by superstar performers like Madonna and David Bowie, Stefani began playing in a band and performing in clubs on the Lower East Side of Manhattan. Eventually, after years of hard work and feeling unsure of herself, she was offered a recording contract that would change her entire life.

While Stefani was working on new music, her record producer started calling her "Gaga" because the notes she sang reminded him of the song "Radio Ga Ga" by the band Queen. She added "Lady" to it and created an unforgettable stage name!

Lady Gaga released her first album in 2008. It was called *The Fame*. People all over the world started singing and dancing to its hit songs "Poker Face," "Just Dance," and "Paparazzi." The album even won a Grammy Award!

Lady Gaga became known for more than just her music. She also has a very fun sense of style. The clothes she wears on- and offstage reflect her one-of-a-kind personality.

She has worn a fluffy blue coat with giant shoulders,

a dress covered in big plastic bath bubbles,

a huge inflatable star,

and even a pair of *very* high heels shaped like armadillos!

With every album she released, Lady Gaga became more and more popular. She loves all her amazing fans and affectionately calls them "Little Monsters."

She feels so lucky to be living her dreams and to offer support to kids who might be going through the same things she did growing up—being bullied and feeling sad.

With the help of her mother, Lady Gaga created the Born This Way Foundation in 2011. Its name comes from the title of one of her hit songs. "Born This Way" is about celebrating what makes each person special. The foundation encourages everyone to practice kindness toward themselves and the people around them.

An incredible music career and an important foundation aren't the only successes Lady Gaga has had. She's also a movie star! Her very first film was called *A Star Is Born,* and it was a smash hit worldwide.

Her performance earned her an Academy Award nomination for Best Actress. She also wrote a song for the movie called "Shallow," and it won the Academy Award for Best Song!

Lady Gaga has become one of the most famous entertainers of all-time, singing every style of music from pop to jazz to country. She has written dozens of hit songs, performed sold-out concerts around the world, worked with legendary musicians like Tony Bennett, and been a dedicated activist for important social issues like equal rights.

Lady Gaga is a true superstar! Not because of the songs she writes and the awards she wins, but because of the encouraging words she shares. Lady Gaga inspires people to love themselves.

"You have to be unique and different and shine in your own way."

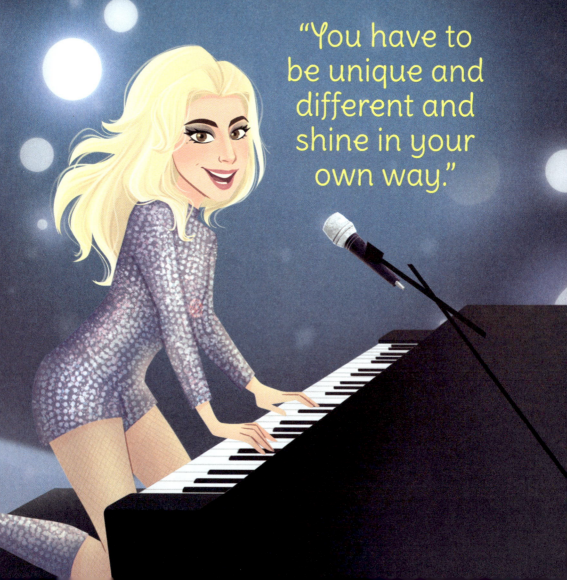